THE SCOTTISH OFFICE CENTRAL RESEARCH UNI

Social Work
Research Findings No. 14

CW00386477

Social Work and Criminal Justice:
Early Arrangements

Lesley McAra

National Objectives and Standards for Social Work Services in the Criminal Justice System and the 100% funding initiative ('the policy') were introduced in 1991[1] in order to secure the provision of services which have the confidence of both criminal justice decision-makers and the wider public. This study is part of the social research programme designed to evaluate policy implementation. It examines the initial responses of key criminal justice decision-makers and Scottish Office officials to early arrangements for policy implementation.

Main findings

■ Three facilitators of implementation were identified: the protection of resources through the funding initiative; the development of specialist services integrated into service delivery systems as a whole; and the framework of the National Standards.

■ Impediments to early implementation included: the change to specialist organisational structives; tensions over the relative priority of services and monitoring; concurrent introduction of other social work policies and the fact that 100% funding arrangements did not cover all services.

■ Sheriff interviewees endorsed the model of criminal justice embedded in the Standards, but when sentencing offenders at high risk of custody, punishment and public protection rather than the quality of social work services were the primary considerations.

■ Sheriffs were generally satisfied with probation services and considered that policy implementation had made a major impact in some areas. Their views on community service, however, were more polarised.

■ Throughcare was believed by Scottish Office officials to be the least well developed service prior to policy implementation and the policy had, thus far, had limited impact.

---

1 National Standards for Community Service had been introduced in 1989

1998

Introduction

The National Objectives and Standards (the Standards, 1991) set out a framework within which local authorities are required to provide social work services where costs are met by the 100 per cent funding initiative (initially, social enquiry reports and associated court services, community service, probation, parole and other aspects of throughcare).

Prior to the development of the Standards, local authorities had to fund most social work services out of their general income. Criminal justice services were, therefore, in competition for resources with other local authority services and as a result were not always of sufficient quantity and quality to meet the requirements of the courts.

The main aims of the policy are:

■ to reduce the use of custody by increasing the availability, improving the quality and targeting the use of community-based court disposals on those most at risk of custody, especially young offenders;

■ to enable offenders to address their offending behaviour and make a successful adjustment to law-abiding life.

The purpose of this study was to examine the initial responses of key criminal justice decision-makers and Scottish Office officials to the principal objectives of the policy and the early arrangements for its implementation.

Findings are based on an analysis of the Standards and interviews in 1992-1993 with: twelve sheriffs (two from each of the six Scottish sheriffdoms); one procurator fiscal from each sheriffdom; two members of the Parole Board for Scotland; and four Scottish Office officials.

Planning and management

The research identified a tension in the policy between the framework of the Standards and the need to develop services within available resources. This is reflected in differences of view between central government officials over: the adequacy of early strategic planning arrangements; and the relative priority given to developing service delivery and the National Core Data System which was established for monitoring purposes.

Three facilitators of policy implementation were identified: the protection of resources through the 100 per cent funding initiative; the development of specialist services integrated into service delivery systems as a whole; and the framework of the National Standards.

Impediments to early implementation included: differing priorities within central government; the policy context; organisational factors; and the nature of the 100% funding initiative.

Sentencing

Three factors were identified as increasing shrieval confidence in a disposal: feedback on the process and outcome of supervision in individual cases; a well written social enquiry report; and guaranteed funding for services. However increased confidence in disposals did not necessarily guarantee that a particular disposal would be used more frequently and may have no part to play in decisions taken about serious categories of offence.

The research found that although sheriffs were willing to endorse the model of criminal justice which informs the Standards, they indicated that, when sentencing offenders at high risk of custody, punishment rather than the nature or quality of social work input to community-based disposals, was a major consideration. They believed that this was compatible with public interest and protection.

Social enquiry reports

The majority of sheriffs commented that there had been major improvements in recent years in social enquiry report writing, especially in respect of the recommendations and conclusions. Reports were generally delivered on time although they were often only available on the morning of the court. Where dissatisfaction was expressed it was because reports contained unnecessary detail and recommendations were sometimes thought by sheriffs to be unrealistic.

Probation

Sheriffs were generally satisfied with the provision of probation services. Implementation of the Standards was considered to have had a major impact in some areas. Greater information was now available about services and the range and quality of programmes were believed to have improved.

Nevertheless, sheriffs generally thought that there was further scope for development of intensive probation projects aimed at offenders at high risk of custody and services aimed at young people involved in less serious offences.

Throughcare

Throughcare was believed to have been the least well developed social work criminal justice service prior to policy implementation and therefore to have the most progress to make. Though some interviewees thought that the quality of prison social work reports and home circumstance reports was variable and linked this to the experience and ability of individual social workers, others thought that the quality had improved, reflecting more thorough input from social workers and increased co-operation between agencies.

The implementation of "Continuity Through Co-operation" a national framework of policy and practice guidance for social work in prisons, (Scottish Prisons Service/Social Work Services Group, 1989) was believed to have enhanced co-operation between different service providers in a number of prison units. However, some interviewees thought that the provision of prison-based social work was patchy and prisoners in some units lacked contact with social workers.

Parole board members considered that they had insufficient information about available community-based services and that better liaison with social work administrators could address this. However, interviewees generally thought that community-based throughcare was improving although there was greater scope for inter-agency collaboration.

Conclusion

Responses of key criminal justice decision-makers to early arrangements for policy implementation would suggest that progress was more advanced in some areas of service delivery than others. These issues have been examined in more detail in the other studies in the research programme.

4

The study was carried out by The Scottish Office Central Research Unit as part of the programme of research to evaluate social work criminal justice policy. The research programme was conducted by The Scottish Office Central Research Unit in collaboration with the Social Work Research Centre at Stirling University and with Edinburgh University. It was funded by the Home Department of The Scottish Office.

Social Work and Criminal Justice Volume 2: 'Early Arrangements'; the report of the research programme summarised in this Research Findings is published by The Stationery Office. It may be purchased from The Stationery Office, price £13 per copy.

Reports of Individual Studies on this programme are also available:

Social Work and Criminal Justice Volume 1: 'The Impact of Policy'.
Social Work and Criminal Justice Volume 3:'The National and Local Context'.
Social Work and Criminal Justice Volume 4:'Sentencer Decision-Making'.
Social Work and Criminal Justice Volume 5:'Parole Board Decision-Making'.
Social Work and Criminal Justice Volume 6:'Probation'.
Social Work and Criminal Justice Volume 7:'Community-Based Throughcare'.

Cheques should be made payable to The Stationery Office and addressed to:

The Stationery Office Ltd, Mail Order Department, 21 South Gyle Crescent, Edinburgh, EH12 9EB. Telephone: 0131-479-3141 or Fax 0131-479-3142.

The following Research Findings for other studies on this programme are also available:

Findings 13:'The Impact of Policy'.
Findings 15: 'The National and Local Context'.
Findings 16: 'Sentencer Decision-Making'.
Findings 17: 'Parole Board Decision-Making'.
Findings 18: 'Probation'.
Findings 19: 'Community-Based Throughcare'.

Research Findings may be photocopied, or further copies may be obtained from:

The Scottish Office Central Research Unit

Room 53

James Craig Walk

Edinburgh EH1 3BA

or

Telephone: 0131-244-5397

Fax: 0131-244-5393

ISBN 0-7480-6660-8

 THE SCOTTISH OFFICE

Designed and produced on behalf of The Scottish Office by The Stationery Office J16005 1/98

9 780748 066605

SOCIAL WORK AND CRIMINAL JUSTICE:

VOLUME 2

VIEWS ON EARLY ARRANGEMENTS FOR POLICY IMPLEMENTATION

Lesley McAra

The Scottish Office Central Research Unit

THE SCOTTISH OFFICE CENTRAL RESEARCH UNIT
1998

ACKNOWLEDGEMENTS

I am indebted to the sheriffs, procurators fiscal, members of the Parole Board for Scotland and Scottish Office officials, who kindly agreed to be interviewed for this study.

I would like to thank Dr Fiona Paterson and Dr Jacqueline Tombs of the Central Research Unit, for their advice and support during the course of the study. Special thanks are also due to Mrs Helen Pinkman for her assistance in transcribing the interview tapes and typing the manuscript.

Lesley McAra
1998

SOCIAL WORK AND CRIMINAL JUSTICE
RESEARCH PROGRAMME REPORTS

Paterson, F. and Tombs, J. (1998)　　　**Social Work and Criminal Justice: Volume 1 -**

　　　　　　　　　　　　　　　　　　　　The Impact of Policy. The Stationery Office.

Phase One:

McAra, L. (1998)　　　　　　　　　　　**Social Work and Criminal Justice: Volume 2 -**

　　　　　　　　　　　　　　　　　　　　Early Arrangements. The Stationery Office.

Phase Two:

Brown, L., Levy, L.　　　　　　　　　　**Social Work and Criminal Justice: Volume 3 -**

and McIvor, G. (1998)　　　　　　　　　*The National and Local Context.* The Stationery Office.

Brown, L., Levy, L. (1998)　　　　　　　**Social Work and Criminal Justice: Volume 4 -**

　　　　　　　　　　　　　　　　　　　　Sentencer Decision Making. The Stationery Office.

McAra, L. (1998a)　　　　　　　　　　　**Social Work and Criminal Justice: Volume 5 -**

　　　　　　　　　　　　　　　　　　　　Parole Board Decision Making. The Stationery Office.

McIvor, G. and　　　　　　　　　　　　**Social Work and Criminal Justice: Volume 6 -**

Barry, M. (1998)　　　　　　　　　　　　*Probation.* The Stationery Office.

McIvor, G. and　　　　　　　　　　　　**Social Work and Criminal Justice: Volume 7 -**

Barry, M. (1998a)　　　　　　　　　　　*Community Based Throughcare.* The Stationery Office.

CONTENTS

SUMMARY

INTRODUCTION

The Policy

In Scotland, statutory social work services to offenders and their families are provided by the local authority social work departments. Since April 1991, the Scottish Office has reimbursed to social work departments the full costs of providing a range of statutory social work services in the criminal justice system. National Objectives and Standards (the National Standards) were introduced by the Social Work Services Group of the Scottish Office to coincide with the introduction of the funding initiative.

The National Standards and the funding initiative cover: social enquiry reports; court social work services; probation; community service; and throughcare (social work services to offenders in prisons is funded by the Scottish Prison Service). Since 1991, the initiative has been extended to supervised release orders, bail information and accommodation schemes, and supervised attendance order schemes (the latter two schemes are not yet available on a national basis).

The main aims of the Government's policy are:

- to reduce the use of custody by increasing the availability, improving the quality and targeting the use of community-based court disposals and throughcare services on those most at risk of custody, especially young adult repeat offenders;

- to enable offenders to address their offending behaviour and make a successful adjustment to law abiding life.

Background to the Research

Central Government's review and evaluation of implementation of the funding initiative and the National Standards involves a programme of inspection by Social Work Services Inspectorate (SWSI), interpretation of statistics and a programme of research.

The research programme is being conducted in three phases and examines progress towards policy objectives. This report is of a preliminary study (Phase One) which examined the perceptions of key criminal justice decision-makers and Scottish Office officials about the principal objectives of the policy and the early arrangements for its implementation. The report is based on analysis of the National Objectives and Standards document and on interviews in 1992-1993 with 12 sheriffs (two from each sheriffdom); one representative of the procurator fiscal service in each sheriffdom; two members of the Parole Board for Scotland; and four Scottish Office officials with senior policy and professional social work responsibility. Their views were obtained on the effectiveness of the implementation of the National Standards; facilitators and inhibitors of implementation; and the impact of early implementation arrangements on sentencers' willingness to make use of non-custodial disposals. The research was undertaken 19 months after the 100 per cent funding arrangements had been implemented.

KEY FINDINGS

Implementation of the National Standards: Central Government Experience

The research identified a tension in the policy between the framework of the objectives and standards and the need to develop services within available resources. In fulfilling its tasks in social work services in the criminal justice system, key concerns of Central Government focused on strategic planning and the National Core Data System.

Strategic Planning

The Central Government social work professional view of strategic planning was that it had a key role to play in enhancing the performance and outcome of local authority services, whereas the administrative view was that it should be primarily finance focused. Variations in responsibility in relation to the policy may at least partly explain different official assessments of the adequacy of policy implementation. The professional view was that strategic planning had progressed well although local authorities required more time to develop planning skills and adequate management information systems. The administrative view however was that it had had limited impact so far and that many local authorities developed plans without sufficient consideration of the availability of Central Government money.

National Core Data System

The National Core Data System was seen as essential to the development of performance and outcome indicators which could help to assess service delivery. Interviewees identified a tension that had arisen between the funding of service delivery and the development of the monitoring system. They agreed that the national core data system had been slow to develop.

Implementation of the National Objectives and Standards: Sentencers' Experiences

Three factors were identified from shrieval interviewees as increasing their confidence in a disposal: feedback on the process and outcome of supervision, a well written social enquiry report and guaranteed funding for services. However, increased confidence in disposals did not appear necessarily to guarantee that a particular disposal would be used more frequently and may have no part to play in decisions taken about serious categories of offence.

The research found a divergence between the aims of the National Objectives and Standards and the sentencing aims of sheriffs. Although sheriffs were willing to endorse the reformative and rehabilitative model of criminal justice which informs the Standards, when sentencing offenders at high risk of custody, punishment rather than the nature or quality of social work input to community based disposals was a major consideration. Sentencers believed that this was compatible with public interest. Sheriffs thought that shifts in sentencing practice away from custody in recent years had been precipitated by court of appeal decisions although they acknowledged that National Standards implementation had contributed to change.

Liaison

Co-operation within Central Government had worked well during the consultation phase of the policy and interviewees were concerned that this level of co-operation should be sustained. Sheriffs and procurators fiscal thought that National Standards implementation had had minimal impact on liaison arrangements and that these were already satisfactory, although procurators fiscal expressed concern about the effectiveness of liaison in cases where a child was the victim.

Local Authority Implementation of Service Standards

Scottish Office interviewees agreed that the local authorities had been slow to implement the policy initially but that it was now being progressed much more quickly.

Three facilitators of policy implementation were identified: the protection of resources through the 100 per cent funding initiative, the development of specialist services integrated into service delivery systems as a whole, and the National Objectives and Standards framework.

There were variations in view as to whether impediments to policy implementation had been organisational factors; differing priorities within Central Government; the policy context within which the policy was being implemented; or the nature of the 100 per cent funding arrangements.

Scottish Office interviewees thought that in the early stages of policy implementation the local authorities had been reluctant to recognise the contribution that the independent sector could make to service provision. Factors in this were thought to be local authority fears about privatisation, the variable quality of independent sector provision, and inexperience on the part of the local authorities in managing the purchaser/provider relationship.

Social Enquiry Reports

The majority of interviewees commented that there had been major improvements in recent years in social enquiry report writing, especially in respect of the recommendations and conclusions. Reports were said to be generally delivered on time although they were often only available on the morning of the court. Interviewees agreed that National Objectives and Standards implementation had contributed to this although other factors mentioned were improvements in social work training (which were believed to have developed over the previous ten years or so) and shifts in attitude on the part of some social workers. Where dissatisfaction was expressed it was because reports contained unnecessary detail and recommendations thought by sheriffs to be unrealistic.

Probation

Sheriffs were generally satisfied with the provision of probation services. National Objectives and Standards implementation was considered to have had a major impact in some areas. Greater information was now available about services and the range and quality of programmes was believed to have improved. Nevertheless, sheriffs generally thought that there was further scope for development. In some areas improvements in services were not attributed to National Objectives and Standards implementation which was seen as having speeded up change already in progress.

Community Service Orders

Interviewees' perception was that the National Objectives and Standards for community service (which have been in place since 1989) had had minimal impact. Most sheriffs thought that community service had always been good in their locality. Others commented that it was poorly supervised and concerns were expressed about the resourcing of services in some areas. Assessments for community service were seen to be of higher quality when undertaken by specialist community service workers. Although some sheriffs wanted to see wider use of community service, others felt that this would undermine the credibility of community service as an alternative to custody and wanted to see the maximum number of hours increased.

Breach of Community Service/Probation Orders

In some areas procurators fiscal believed that social workers lacked knowledge about requirements for breach procedures. In areas where breach procedures worked well, liaison was identified as contributing to this.

Services for Young Adult Offenders

National Objectives and Standards implementation was considered to have had minimal impact on the development of specialist schemes, although a wide range of services were developed prior to implementation and this was continuing. Intensive probation was viewed favourably. However, concerns were expressed that insufficient attention had been given to the development of schemes aimed at young people involved in less serious offences.

Throughcare

Throughcare was believed to be the least well developed social work criminal justice service prior to policy implementation and therefore had the most progress to make.

Reports

Though some interviewees thought that the quality of home circumstance reports and prison social work reports was variable and linked this to the experience and ability of individual social workers, others thought that the quality of reports had improved, reflecting more thorough input from social workers and increased co-operation between agencies.

Social Work Services in Prisons

The implementation of the guidance in *Continuity through Co-operation* was thought to have enhanced co-operation between different service providers in a number of prison units. Although in some areas increased levels of counselling were said to have enhanced prison based social work, some interviewees thought the provision of this service was patchy and prisoners in some units lacked contact with social workers.

Community Based Social Work Services

Parole Board members interviewed thought they had insufficient information about available services and commented that better liaison with social work administrators could address this. Interviewees considered that community based social work services were improving although there was greater scope for inter-agency collaboration. There were variations in view as to the extent to which the independent sector and local authorities should be involved in service provision.

EARLY ARRANGEMENTS

The key findings of this report on the early arrangements for policy implementation will be explored in detail at Phase Two of the evaluation which looks at the impact of the policy on the process and effectiveness of service provision.

CHAPTER ONE

EVALUATION OF THE NATIONAL OBJECTIVES AND STANDARDS AND THE 100 PER CENT FUNDING INITIATIVE

INTRODUCTION

In Scotland, statutory social work services to offenders and their families are provided by the local authority social work departments. Since April 1991, the Scottish Office has reimbursed to social work departments the full costs of providing a range of statutory social work services in the criminal justice system. National Objectives and Standards (the National Standards) were introduced by the Social Work Services Group of the Scottish Office to coincide with the introduction of the funding initiative. The aim of the National Standards is to promote the development of high quality management and practice, the most efficient and effective use of resources, and to provide social work services to the criminal justice system which have the confidence of both the courts and the wider public.

The National Standards and the funding initiative cover: social enquiry reports; court social work services; probation; community service[1]; and throughcare (social work services in prisons is funded by the Scottish Prison Service). Since 1991, the initiative has been extended to supervised release orders, bail information and accommodation schemes, and supervised attendance order schemes (the latter two schemes are not yet available on a national basis). It is intended to include diversion from prosecution in the 100 per cent funding arrangement, subject to the progress of pilot schemes established in 1996. At present, fine supervision means enquiry reports and deferred sentence supervision are not included in the funding initiative.

Prior to the introduction of the 100 per cent funding initiative and the National Standards, local authorities had to fund the majority of social work services out of their general income[2]. Criminal justice services were, therefore, in competition for resources with other local authority services and as a result were not always of sufficient quantity and quality to meet the requirements of the courts.

The main aims of the Government's policy are[3]:

- to reduce the use of custody by increasing the availability, improving the quality and targeting the use of community-based court disposals and throughcare services on those most at risk of custody, especially young adult repeat offenders;

- to enable offenders to address their offending behaviour and make a successful adjustment to law abiding life.

Administration, Review and Planning

The National Objectives and Standards map out new roles for Central Government and the local authorities with regard to the administration, review and planning of the policy.

As part of the policy it is the responsibility of Central Government to review, in consultation with local authorities, the general organisation and management of social work services, the national objectives, priorities and standards as well as the funding arrangements. To assist with the review Central Government is developing a national core data system in consultation with local authorities and other interested parties. The national core data system will inform Central Government evaluation strategies and policy and resource planning. It will also assist local service planning, management and oversight of service provision[4].

In addition to this, Social Work Services Group (SWSG) has the responsibility (subject to Ministerial and Parliamentary approval) to advise on and determine the level of resources required to meet the standards, to provide funding for those services eligible for 100 per cent grant, and to administer this grant.

National Objectives and Standards implementation coincided with the establishment of the Social Work Inspectorate[5] who have been given, inter alia, the task of monitoring and evaluating the implementation and

---

1   The 100 per cent funding initiative and National Objectives and Standards were first applied to community service in 1989.

2   A brief history of the development of the National Standards and the 100 per cent funding initiative is outlined in Annex I.

3   Evaluation Strategy Working Group, September 1990. More recent statements (the 1996 White Paper on Crime and Punishment, paragraphs 9.1 and 10.3) are consistent with these aims.

4   National Objectives and Standards for Social Work Services in the Criminal Justice System: Central and Local Government Tasks: Paragraph 34.

5   The Social Work Inspectorate was established in April 1992 at the same time as the service standards were being implemented and one year after the implementation of the 100 per cent funding arrangements. The Inspectorate comprises teams of social work professionals who were formerly social work advisers with SWSG. One team of inspectors is responsible for inspecting social work services in the criminal justice system and continuing policy advice within SWSG.

operation of the National Objectives priorities and Standards. One of their key functions is to review the performance and outcomes of services provided by local authorities and other agencies.

As a result of National Objectives and Standards implementation, local authorities now have the responsibility to provide services which meet National Objectives' and Standards' requirements. In response to the policy, they have also had to develop organisational structures directed towards achieving a cohesive approach to service delivery. A key feature which the government considers necessary to deliver effective services is the appointment of specialist staff who are devoted to criminal justice work, and the appointment of sufficient staff at each organisational level. As a consequence, local authorities also have to develop education and training strategies.

In addition to this, local authorities are now required to develop, implement and review strategic plans. These plans should be aligned and integrated with policy planning for other social work services provided by the local authorities and should be developed within a framework of national priorities laid down annually by SWSG[6]. In particular they should focus on the most efficient and effective use of resources, should reflect the contribution that other agencies at both national and local level can make to service provision, and should assist managers and practitioners to measure both performance and outcome. The strategic plans have to be developed in consultation with other service providers such as the independent sector and service users. In conjunction with strategic planning provisions the authorities have to devise localised systems for monitoring and evaluating policy implementation.

Strategic plans must reflect the contribution which independent sector organisations may make to service provision. Where independent sector agencies are involved in service provision, they too have to meet the requirements of the National Objectives and Standards, to devise methods of monitoring and evaluating their own performance and also to develop systems for their own training.

The evaluation of the policy will need to consider the adequacy of the new organisational, management and financial arrangements that have been established and their impact upon both service performance and outcome.

BACKGROUND TO THE RESEARCH

Central Government's review and evaluation of implementation of the funding initiative and the National Standards involves a programme of inspection by Social Work Services Inspectorate (SWSI), interpretation of statistics and a programme of research.

The research programme has three phases. The main purpose of Phase One, which was undertaken in 1992-1993, was to examine the responses of key criminal justice decision makers and Scottish Office officials to the principal objectives of the policy and the early arrangements for its implementation (McAra, 1998). Phase Two consists of five inter-related studies, conducted in 1994-1995, which examine progress towards policy objectives: the national and local context of policy implementation (Brown, Levy and McIvor, 1998); sentencer decision making (Brown and Levy, 1998); Parole Board decision making (McAra, 1998a); the process and outcomes of probation (McIvor and Barry, 1998); and the process and outcomes of throughcare (McIvor and Barry, 1998a). Phase Three will look at the longer term impact of services for offenders.

Aims and Objectives

The first phase examines the degree to which the funding initiative, as implemented by local authorities, is perceived to be meeting the first of the main objectives: to reduce the use of custody by increasing the availability, improving the quality and targeting the use of community based disposals and throughcare services on those most at risk of custody, particularly young adult repeat offenders. This study examines the perceptions and responses of key decision makers within the criminal justice system and Central Government to early arrangements for implementation of the policy.

The objectives of the research are to examine the attitudes of sentencers, prosecutors, Parole Board members and Scottish Office officials to the objectives of the funding initiative; the means by which the objectives are to be achieved; the levels of success of early arrangements for their implementation and to provide a baseline for Phase Two of the research.

The report was written in 1993 and includes:

- an assessment of the perceived effectiveness of the implementation of the National Objectives and Standards;

---

6 The strategic planning system was being reviewed, at the time of writing (1993), in consultation with the Convention of Scottish Local Authorities.

- identification of perceived facilitators and inhibitors of National Objectives and Standards implementation;
- an assessment of the impact of early arrangements for the implementation of the National Objectives and Standards on sentencers' willingness to make use of non-custodial disposals.

Method

The research involved an analysis of the National Objectives and Standards document and semi-structured interviews, each lasting approximately 45 minutes, with key criminal justice decision makers and Scottish Office officials. Interviews were conducted with twelve sheriffs, two sheriffs from each sheriffdom, including sheriffs who were involved in the consultation phase of National Objectives and Standards development and sheriffs who were not. Interviews were also conducted with one representative of the procurator fiscal service in each sheriffdom and two members of the Parole Board for Scotland. In addition to this, four Scottish Office officials with senior policy and professional social work responsibility were interviewed.

Themes Discussed in Interview

Interviewees were asked for their responses to the policy objectives; the model of social work practice informing the policy and their assessment of early arrangements for policy implementation. Procurators fiscal declined to answer questions on the objectives of the policy and the model of social work practice informing the policy as they felt these were not matters appropriate for prosecutor comment.

In addition to this, interviewees were asked about areas of concern specific to their role within the criminal justice system: sheriffs were asked about the impact of National Standards on sentencing options; procurators fiscal were asked to comment on the impact of the policy on breach proceedings; Parole Board members were asked about the impact of the policy on prison based and community based components of throughcare. Scottish Office officials were asked for their views on the issues for Central Government in fulfilling its tasks as designated by the National Objectives and Standards.

Structure of the Report

Part I of the report examines Central Government and sentencers' experiences of the implementation of the National Objectives and Standards and the nature of liaison arrangements between key agents in the criminal justice system. Part II examines responses to service provision and includes a review of responses to: local authority implementation of service standards; social enquiry reports; community based disposals and throughcare.

PART I

EXPERIENCE OF IMPLEMENTING THE NATIONAL OBJECTIVES AND STANDARDS

CHAPTER TWO

IMPLEMENTATION OF NATIONAL OBJECTIVES AND STANDARDS: CENTRAL GOVERNMENT EXPERIENCE

INTRODUCTION

The National Objectives and Standards outline a series of tasks which Central Government has to undertake. In order to identify inhibitors and facilitators of policy implementation it is essential to examine the issues for Central Government in fulfilling these tasks to date. Two aspects of these tasks are concerned with the funding of the policy and policy monitoring and review. The key issues raised by Central Government interviewees were the role of local authority strategic planning in relation to the funding of the policy, and the development of the national core data system in relation to policy monitoring and review. Variation in views expressed on these issues were associated with different responsibilities in relation to the policy. These views reflect the potential for tension within the policy itself between the framework of the objectives and standards and the elements of the policy which highlight the need to develop services within available resources.

STRATEGIC PLANNING

The main purposes of the strategic plans which local authorities are required to develop on a three year planning cycle are: to ensure the most effective and efficient use of financial and other resources; to assist with service development; and to provide a means of measuring performance and outcome. Central Government has the responsibility of reviewing and refining these plans in consultation with local authorities[7].

There were mixed responses amongst interviewees when they were asked to consider the extent to which the planning process had been successfully implemented. From the professional perspective, the local authorities had progressed well with the planning process given the limited amount of time it had been in operation. Effective planning depended on local authorities gaining the necessary planning skills and it was felt that greater experience would increase competence. The potential for improved planning was inhibited by inadequate development of management information systems which could provide the necessary data from which to review both finance and service elements.

The administrative view of the way in which strategic planning had operated in practice was less positive. It was felt that local authorities did not give sufficient consideration to the availability of Central Government money when they developed their plans.

Two aspects of the policy were considered to have contributed to this problem. In part it may have arisen because of the nature of 100 per cent funding in itself. Where authorities know that government will pay the full cost of certain specified services, there may be a temptation to plan a more elaborate version of the services rather than one which is more limited in scope. It was recognised though that, despite the statement within the National Objectives and Standards that service development should be within "available resources", in general the objectives and standards had been necessarily developed without detailed costings being available. The Objectives and Standards were then implemented in a policy context where close attention had to be paid to costs and financial constraints.

Despite the agreed importance in principle of strategic planning within the overall policy, it was accordingly recognised that, in practice, financial constraints may have inhibited the effectiveness of the early strategic planning process.

Underlying Views of Strategic Planning

The responses of officials to early attempts at strategic planning by local authorities are linked to their different responsibilities in relation to the policy.

The professional view was that strategic planning should be placed at the heart of service development. Strategic planning was believed to assist rather than inhibit financial planning, particularly when cash limits exist. It was also considered to be an exercise in promoting accountability because it required local authorities to clarify their objectives, and develop performance targets and systems for measuring them. Fully developed strategic planning systems, it was believed, should lead to improvements in both performance and outcome.

What was sought was the development of effective services, that is, services which would have an impact on

---

[7] The strategic planning system was being reviewed, at the time of writing (1993), in consultation with the Convention of Scottish Local Authorities.

offending behaviour. The development of programmes which tackle the needs of small groups of high risk offenders such as sex offenders or violent offenders, was seen to be essential. Concern was expressed that the financial constraints within which the policy operated would mean that groups such as these could be overlooked:

> "The National Standards are about quality as well as quantity. The danger is that when you have resource constraints you go for quantity and to a far less extent than you ought, quality. You may get lots of people on supervision, but if you do not provide the programmes and inputs which are necessary to tackle offending behaviour you are not going to achieve the objective of reducing offending behaviour." (Professional)

It was recognised that there were tensions in the strategic planning process between the provision of services focused on need and resource availability. This tension was felt to be inevitable and therefore had to be managed. One way of managing the tension was to incorporate a requirement on local authorities to examine the scope for efficiency in their plans.

The official involved in the administration of the policy viewed effective strategic planning primarily as necessarily finance focused. The financial resources available for criminal justice services are set by Parliament. The official defined plans as being less successfully developed where local authorities did not properly reflect the agenda of financial constraint and cost effectiveness.

NATIONAL CORE DATA SYSTEM

The development of the National Core Data System is one of the tasks outlined in the Objectives and Standards which has to be undertaken by Central Government in consultation with the local authorities and other interested parties. The primary function of the National Core Data System is to produce a database for the purpose of monitoring and evaluating the policy; assessing the impact of new arrangements; and assisting policy and resource planning.

Although the implementation of other elements of the policy was subject to careful planning, there had been no coherent implementation plan for the national core data system. There was consensus amongst interviewees that it had faced particularly acute teething problems and had been slow to develop. This had been caused by a number of factors: negotiations with local authorities about the form in which the data should be collected had been protracted; delays had been caused by union disputes in certain areas; substantial time had also been devoted to the development and piloting of the unit return forms on which the system was based. In addition to this, the implementation of the Objectives and Standards had proceeded at a faster rate in some authorities than in others.

Interviewees identified a tension that had arisen between the financing of service delivery and the development of the monitoring system. Because of financial constraints, it had been necessary to make a choice between putting money into the provision of services or into monitoring. It had been felt that it would be inappropriate to ration service delivery in order to set up the monitoring system and that the cost of providing the unit returns (on which the system was based) was prohibitive:

> "I wouldn't like to tell the court, 'I'm sorry ... there is no probation this week because we're paying for the forms'." (Administrator)

Nevertheless it was believed that without adequate management information systems it would be difficult to monitor and evaluate policy implementation effectively. The primary purpose of the database was to deliver evidence of efficiency, effectiveness and how well services were targeted and it had a key role to play in the development of performance and outcome indicators. One view was that when the tension had arisen between financing services and developing the database, the development of the data system should have been given greater priority:

> "...unequivocally there comes a time, if you have to make a choice of allocating more money for more service delivery or give that money to ensure that adequate management information systems are in place, the decision has to be in favour of the latter not the former, because you will cut off your nose to spite your face if you do not." (Professional)

CONCLUSION

The different responsibilities of interviewees in relation to policy implementation may largely account for the variations in priority which they assigned to particular elements of the policy. These variations in priority help to explain different official assessments of the adequacy of policy implementation. They also reflect the tensions between costs and the quality and scope of service provision which lie at the heart of the policy itself.

Interviewee responses suggest that the tensions in the policy need to be recognised explicitly when local authority performance in implementing the service Objectives and Standards is monitored and evaluated. When resources are limited it is important to give clear signals as to where priorities should lie. The review of the strategic planning process (which is underway at the time of writing) and any future review of the service Objectives and Standards provide opportunities to consider: how the planning process can contribute to the effective management of these tensions, and to examine in detail the relationship between costs of services and indicators of service quality.

CHAPTER THREE

IMPLEMENTATION OF THE NATIONAL OBJECTIVES AND STANDARDS: SENTENCERS' EXPERIENCES

INTRODUCTION

One of the principal objectives of the policy is to reduce the use of custody by increasing the availability, improving the quality and targeting the use of community based disposals on those most at risk of custody, especially young adult repeat offenders.

This objective presupposes that sentencers' decision making is informed in part by their assessment of what social work services can provide. If the quality of social work services can be assured and its effectiveness demonstrated, the policy assumes that this will persuade sentencers to use non-custodial disposals in cases in which otherwise they might have imposed a custodial sentence.

The National Objectives and Standards for probation and throughcare services, together with the guidance on effective policy and practice in social work supervision included in the policy, are underpinned by a reformative and rehabilitative model of criminal justice. The policy and practice guidance advocates the development of programmes which focus on offending behaviour, tackle behaviour associated with offending and address offenders' underlying problems. Control of the offender and the management of risk, key priorities in the development of effective community based programmes, are to be accomplished within this reformative and rehabilitative framework.

Community service differs from probation in that it is primarily punitive and reparative rather than reformative - the punitive element is contained in the number of hours the offender has to devote to the work, the discipline of the work and in the procedures available for non-compliance[8]. Nevertheless the objectives and standards for community service are underpinned by a broadly rehabilitative approach. For example the standards state that community service schemes should seek to offer work places of value to the individual offender which will also enhance their social responsibility and self-respect. In addition schemes should offer access to advice and help with personal, domestic or family problems which may interfere with the successful completion of an order. Moreover, by seeking to deal with more serious and persistent offenders in a non-custodial setting (as community service does), the policy aims to avoid or reduce disruption to family ties and work prospects[9], key features of a rehabilitative model of criminal justice.

The impact of the National Objectives and Standards on sentencing decisions is likely to be affected, in part, by the extent to which sheriffs deem the reformative and rehabilitative framework of the National Objectives and Standards to be an appropriate model for dealing with the high custody risk offender groups, including young adult repeat offenders, on which the policy aims to target services. In order to explore these issues, sheriffs were asked about sentencing aims and decisions including those for high risk offender groups.

SENTENCING PERSPECTIVES

Sheriffs were reluctant to identify themselves as adopting a particular perspective when sentencing. Most saw themselves as having their own particular decision-making framework made up of a disparate set of aims, factors and competing philosophies, elements of which could be used in specific cases:

"It's a recipe which you can vary the ingredients according to the particular facts of a case." (Sheriff)

Factors commonly mentioned as contributing to decisions were the nature of an offence, the background and circumstances of an accused and an accused's record. Generally sheriffs' views on sentencing aims indicated that they were concerned to reduce the incidence of crime, to punish, to reform and to deter, according to the circumstances of particular cases. These aims have different implications for the potential impact of a policy directed broadly towards reform and rehabilitation.

However when sheriffs were asked to consider sentencing aims and practice in more detail, their responses were less pragmatic. Interviewees were asked to comment on the rehabilitative and reformative model of

---

[8] Social Work Services Group (1991). *The National Objectives and Standards for Social Work Services in the Criminal Justice System: Community Service:* paragraph 10. The Scottish Office.

[9] Social Work Services Group. *Social Work Supervision: Towards Effective Policy and Practice: A Supplement to the National Objectives and Standards for Social Work Services in the Criminal Justice System.* The Scottish Office. Paragraphs 1 and 2.

criminal justice which informed the standards and, in particular, to comment on the emphasis on tackling offending behaviour and addressing offenders' underlying problems. A common view was that these were worthy aims which should inform and guide sentencing decisions:

"These are the things that sentencing is all about." (Sheriff)

Nevertheless when sheriffs addressed sentencing issues in relation to specific categories of offender, they were neither pragmatic nor did they adhere to the principles of a reformative and rehabilitative model of criminal justice. An example of this was the sentencing of high risk offenders.

Sentencing Options for High Custody Risk Offenders

The National Objectives and Standards are in part directed towards the encouragement of the use of non-custodial disposals, where appropriate, for more serious categories of offender. Sheriffs were asked about the extent to which the early arrangements for the implementation of the policy had impacted on their sentencing of offenders most at risk of custody.

Most sheriffs did not expect that the implementation of the National Standards would result in a significant difference in the numbers of custodial sentences. In their view the number of high risk offenders who could safely be diverted from custody was small and there was little scope for increase. A common view was that in many cases the gravity of the offence was such that anything other than a custodial sentence was out of the question. Most interviewees had a base-line for offences which merited custody and it was generally expected that National Objectives and Standards implementation would have minimal impact on this. The key factor determining the position of this base-line was held to be the public interest.

Sheriffs generally considered that they only gave custodial sentences when this was in the public interest. In their responses no links were made between the concept of the public interest and the use of non-custodial disposals. The public interest was conceived both as protection of the public and maintenance of public confidence in the law. The public perception of sentencing practice was seen as being a key factor in the maintenance of public confidence:

"You have to keep an element of punishment because society expects that. If you do not punish you get things like vigilantes taking the law into their own hands and the law would go into disrepute." (Sheriff)

Many sheriffs stated that the public expected custodial disposals for high risk offenders; some sheriffs went as far as to say that if they discerned a shift in public opinion they would be encouraged to make greater use of community-based disposals. However one interviewee commented that the media had played a significant role in constructing public perception of serious offenders:

"It's a public relations thing. If the public became less worried - public worry is artificially manufactured. The media have a lot to answer for there." (Sheriff)

These responses indicate that it may be difficult for National Objectives and Standards implementation to have an impact on shrieval decision making on more serious categories of offender. The policy aims to enable more serious categories of offender to be dealt with in a community based setting by the development of programmes which are directed towards reducing risk. However, the sheriffs indicated that their sentencing responses in such cases were not determined by an assessment of what social work services can provide but by their interpretation of public interest. This interpretation is in turn influenced by factors such as the media, over which social work managers and practitioners have no control.

Sentencing Options for Young Adult Offenders

The National Objectives and Standards lay emphasis on the development of services for young adult offenders:

"The development and provision of services for young adult offenders should be complemented by the development and provision of services to the children's hearings so that a full range of options is open to the courts and the children's hearings for dealing with 15-17 year old offenders." (National Standards, General Issues, paragraph 10).

At present the judiciary are the gate-keepers to the children's hearings system for young adult offenders who are between the ages of 16 and 17 years six months and who are not subject to a current supervision order. The court has the power to remit such cases to the children's hearings for advice or disposal. However, the National Objectives and Standards documents points out that these powers are not widely used. (National Standards, General Issues, paragraph 103.)

To explore the questions of sentencing options for young adult offenders and the role of the judiciary in relation to the children's hearings system, sheriffs were asked about the use of their discretionary powers and about the appropriateness of dealing with young adult repeat offenders in the criminal justice system.

The majority of sheriffs interviewed said that they never remitted offenders to children's hearings because they felt that hearings were not able to offer constructive solutions to the problems that such offenders posed. The hearings system was variously described as having "no teeth" and as being a "soft option".

Most of those who did remit cases commented that they did not do so frequently. These sheriffs tended to remit only minor offences where they believed the offender would be more likely to benefit from the advice and guidance provided in the hearings system rather than that provided by a probation order. An example of the type of cases in which it was thought appropriate to remit the offender was where the criminal element was outweighed by the social problems that the offender faced, in particular where there were family background problems, where the offender was very immature or where there was insufficient parental guidance. In their view the major benefit of the children's hearing system was that parents could be involved in the decisions that were made.

Most of the sheriffs interviewed did not believe that the scope of the children's hearings should be widened. As highlighted above, this was primarily because the hearings were not seen as offering a constructive alternative for responding to young adult offenders. Underpinning this view were clear concerns about public and offender perceptions of the hearings system.

Both the public and young adult offenders were also believed to perceive the hearings system as a "soft option". Being dealt with in the criminal justice system was felt to impress upon young adult offenders the seriousness of their offending behaviour. This was primarily because of the court's power to use custodial sentences. It was generally believed that the public had more confidence in the criminal justice system in dealing with this group of offenders because the criminal justice system could be properly punitive. Many sheriffs took a pessimistic view of young adult male offenders, believing that there was a high incidence of "wickedness" amongst this group and that much of their behaviour was as a consequence intractable.

In this context it would appear difficult for National Objectives and Standards to have a major impact on sentencing decisions for high risk young adult offenders. Even in less serious cases of young adult offenders, many sheriffs believed that they had a duty to punish and as a consequence a punitive approach appeared to inform the decisions that they made.

Social work services that are developed specifically for young adult offenders may only prove attractive to sheriffs if it can be demonstrated that they are able to control the behaviour of this group and that any risk is managed effectively. It was generally felt that the policy was at too early a stage of implementation for any demonstrable impact on decision making to have occurred.

IMPACT OF DISPOSALS ON SENTENCING DECISIONS

As highlighted in the introduction to this chapter, the National Objectives and Standards assume that if the quality of social work services can be assured and its longer term effectiveness demonstrated, sheriffs will be persuaded to make greater use of non-custodial sentences in cases where otherwise a custodial disposal would be imposed. Sheriffs were asked about the factors that increased their confidence in a disposal and what impact increased confidence had on the decisions that they take.

Three main factors were identified as influencing confidence in a disposal: quality of feedback on the progress and outcome of supervision; quality of social enquiry reports; guaranteed funding for service provision.

Feedback

The feedback that sheriffs received on supervision took the form of final reports on completion of an order, breach reports in the event of non-compliance with an order and, on occasions, review reports on the progress of an order. Sheriffs generally considered that the quality of feedback had an impact on their decisions. One sheriff commented that if there was "a good after sales service" they would be more likely to "buy the product". In particular, breach reports were viewed favourably as evidence of rigorous enforcement of an order and this enhanced rather than undermined shrieval confidence in the supervising officer and in the disposal. Aside from breach reports, it is not clear from shrieval responses what the nature of the most appropriate form of feedback would be. Many sheriffs had inconsistent views on feedback. While it was generally recognised that feedback enhanced confidence, several sheriffs pointed out that it was not feasible for feedback to be provided for every case and that they did not have the time to read a large volume of reports. A minority of sheriffs did not want any feedback in whatever form.

Social Enquiry Reports

Well written social enquiry reports enhanced confidence in disposals because they gave detailed information about the arrangements for supervising an offender and set out the components of action plans or work placements. The impact of social enquiry reports on sentencing practice was, however, an area of controversy.

Several sheriffs commented that social enquiry reports were helpful in cases where they were considering a non-custodial disposal, with one interviewee going as far as saying that, because the court now had more confidence in reports, this had shifted the burden of sentencing. The court was becoming even more dependent upon the report for guidance and, given that they were predisposed to accept this guidance, there was less of a need for a plea in mitigation. The sheriff claimed that this had speeded up the whole process of sentencing, thereby saving time and money.

For some sheriffs the key role played by social enquiry reports in sentencing was that they were based on independent sources of information against which a plea in mitigation could be checked. This function of social enquiry reports is markedly different from that outlined in the National Objectives and Standards which state that the primary purpose of the social enquiry report is to act as an aid to sentencing.

In more serious cases where custody was believed to be a "foregone conclusion", sheriffs tended to ask for a report only because it was a statutory requirement. In cases such as these the reports had no impact on decisions taken.

A greater impact of social enquiry reports on sentencing was not always perceived positively and some interviewees believed that social workers were now taking too active a role in the sentencing process. This was particularly the case when reports which recommended a community based disposal were used in appeals against a custodial sentence:

> "Social workers must not be allowed to make it more difficult for sentencers to impose a custodial sentence." (Sheriff)

Guaranteed Funding for Services

Guaranteed funding for services enhanced shrieval confidence as they felt it would secure consistent and well resourced service provision. The extent to which resourcing of service provision had an impact on shrieval decision making was a contested issue. A common theme was that financial or economic considerations should play no part in the sentencing process. However, some sheriffs acknowledged that if there were major resource constraints on a service, which meant that it could not be properly administered, they would not consider using it. Several sheriffs had in the past been forced to choose what they perceived as a weaker alternative to their preferred disposal because of financial constraints. Some interviewees said that they had on occasions given a probation order instead of community service to a high custody risk offender or had used deferred sentence instead of probation.

Overall, information about the nature and outcome of supervision is one of the key factors which determines the level of confidence a sheriff may have in a community based disposal. Interviewees' responses indicated that this factor has had a variable impact on decisions made thus far. This implies that increased confidence in a disposal may not always guarantee that the disposal will be used more frequently. Significantly, the responses to the impact of social enquiry reports on sentencing suggest that confidence in a disposal may have no part to play in decisions made about more serious categories of offence.

NATIONAL OBJECTIVES AND STANDARDS' IMPACT

The three factors governing confidence in a disposal - feedback, social enquiry reports and guaranteed funding - are areas on which the National Objectives and Standards and the 100 per cent funding initiative are targeted. Sheriffs were asked to consider the extent to which they expected that National Standards would have an impact on the decisions that they made.

A common perception was that the National Objectives and Standards had had no major effect on sentencing practice. This was because there had already been a shift in sentencing practice away from custody over a number of years and this had been precipitated by court of appeal decisions. In tandem with this shift, there had already been some increase in the perceived overall quality of social work services. Sheriffs interviewed accordingly generally considered the National Objectives and Standards to be contributing to change rather than to be a primary cause of it. A minority of sheriffs viewed the National Objectives and Standards primarily as a social work rather than a criminal justice policy. If services improved as a result of policy implementation they considered this would be of some benefit to the court. But these sheriffs considered that the objectives and standards ought not in any case to have any impact on sentencing because that was the prerogative of sentencers.

"I don't pay any attention to anything seeking to influence me - I decide what is just and proper in a particular case." (Sheriff)

"I decide - the National Standards are not meant to have an effect on sentencing." (Sheriff)

CONCLUSION

As highlighted in the introduction to this chapter, a central tenet of the National Objectives and Standards is that sheriffs may be persuaded to consider the use of community disposals more often if the quality of social work services can be assured.

Nevertheless interviewee responses indicate that it may be difficult for the National Objectives and Standards to impact on sheriffs' willingness to make greater use of non-custodial disposals. In principle sheriffs did not identify themselves as adopting a particular theoretical perspective on sentencing, although when asked about the aims of the policy they were willing to endorse them. When discussing sentencing in general, sheriffs described a pragmatic approach to decision making. However, when questioned on responses to serious offenders and young adult offenders, key policy targets, their accounts of sentencing were more consistent with a punitive approach. This was in part informed by shrieval conceptions of public opinion and interest, neither of which is directly influenced by the nature of social work services.

Sheriffs interviewed indicated that increased confidence in a disposal does not always guarantee that it will be used more frequently. Greater uptake of community based disposals may therefore depend upon shifts in shrieval conceptions of public interest, and in their perspectives on the ability of social work programmes to impact on the behaviour of young adult male offenders. This suggests that, despite the negative views on feedback expressed by a minority of interviewees, provision of information on the outcome of community based social work supervision will have a key role to play in enhancing the use of non-custodial disposals.

CHAPTER FOUR
LIAISON

INTRODUCTION

The National Objectives and Standards state that it is essential for social work departments to develop effective liaison arrangements with sentencers and agencies working in the criminal justice system. The range of tasks which the policy lays down for Central Government and local authorities requires wide ranging consultation between institutions. The purpose of these arrangements is to enhance the effectiveness of social work contributions to the criminal justice system and to assist in fulfilling the key objectives of the policy.

This chapter explores the nature of the relationship between the criminal justice system and social work; how those holding key positions define good and effective liaison; the range and perceived effectiveness of liaison arrangements; and the extent to which the National Objectives and Standards were perceived to have had an impact on these.

CO-OPERATION WITHIN CENTRAL GOVERNMENT

Chapter Two discussed the variation in views expressed by Scottish Office officials involved in the implementation, administration and review of the National Objectives and Standards. Views were sought on the degree of co-operation between different groups within the Scottish Office.

There was a consensus among the interviewees that the consultation process prior to policy implementation had worked well:

> "An impressive result, an example of good co-operation between the professions." (Administrator)

One key concern was to sustain the interest of criminal justice officials who did not have direct responsibility for administering the policy. The issue was defined as one of "ownership". The National Objectives and Standards were considered to be a shared criminal justice and social work policy rather than purely a social work policy. Unless this was recognised by both social work and criminal justice administrators the interviewee believed that government policy for dealing with crime would arguably be uncoordinated and fragmented.

There were differences of views amongst criminal justice officials about the importance of continued liaison. Parole administrators considered that social work administrators were able to represent their interests adequately and therefore there was no need for greater contact. However, criminal justice administrators felt that they had a key role to play in policy development but considered that they did not receive sufficient information about the progress of policy implementation from SWSG. They saw the benefits of a more structured series of meetings with social work administrators and professionals and also more regular and detailed reports on the way in which the policy was being monitored and evaluated.

A common view amongst interviewees was that the Main Consultation Group comprising Scottish Office officials, representatives from the judiciary and other interested agencies, which meets on an annual basis, should be convened more regularly[10].

SHRIEVAL RESPONSES TO LIAISON ARRANGEMENTS
Liaison Arrangements

Shrieval responses indicate that there is a variety of liaison arrangements across social work authorities. In most social work authorities there is a two-tier arrangement. At regional[11] level there are meetings between sheriffs, the director of social work and social work managers; there are local arrangements within each court where the court liaison officer and other social workers meet sheriffs as and when particular problems or issues arise. In other social work authorities there is an additional level of liaison, comprising formal meetings between sheriffs and middle managers. In one of these areas social workers now attend the local consultative

---

[10] The fieldwork for the study was completed in March 1993. The minutes of the November 1993 meeting of the Main Consultation Group indicate that the issue of more frequent meetings was raised but that members decided to continue to meet on an annual basis.

[11] At the time of this study there were 12 regional social work authorities. Following local government re-organisation in 1996 there are 32 local authorities each with its own social work department.

committee at the sheriff court, at which sheriffs and other criminal justice agents such as the police and procurators fiscal are represented.

Only one interviewee reported that they were not aware of formal arrangements with social work in their area. The only known contact with social workers was said to be ad hoc and through the court based social workers.

Information Received

The kinds of information that sheriffs received from these liaison arrangements varied. At the local level and middle tier levels the main information given and issues discussed concerned outcome of disposals, breach proceedings, new community service order and probation schemes. A minority of interviewees also received statistical information about court sentencing practice which they found useful. The middle tier arrangements also included discussions of broader issues of service delivery, strategic planning of services and resources, though these were more commonly a feature of regional level meetings. Where no middle tier existed the regional level consultation included discussion of local issues in addition to strategic issues.

Impact of National Objectives and Standards

Shrieval responses were sought on the degree to which the nature of liaison had changed since the implementation of the National Objectives and Standards. The majority of interviewees felt that there had been no changes in arrangements. In three areas, however, the National Objectives and Standards had led to the formalisation of previously existing arrangements at either the regional level or at middle management level.

The National Objectives and Standards were believed to have had more impact on the nature of the issues discussed at liaison meetings. Policy implementation had focused discussions by making sheriffs more aware of the availability and nature of social work services. It had also given the issue of alternatives to custody for high risk offenders an increased prominence in discussion.

All of the sheriffs expressed a high degree of satisfaction with current arrangements even in the area where there was no awareness of any formalised liaison arrangements. Only one interviewee wanted to see further changes in arrangements in their area. This interviewee felt that liaison could be made even more effective if a sheriff from each court was nominated as a liaison officer to work with a member of each social work department. At present the organisation and management of social work services in their area were being restructured as a result of National Objectives and Standards implementation. It was felt that the restructuring process had hindered the development of better quality liaison arrangements.

The Benefits of Liaison

Aside from the provision of information, most interviewees considered that the main benefit of liaison was in assisting sheriffs and social workers to understand the others' thinking:

> "It helps me to understand the pressures that they are working under." (Sheriff)

> "Good liaison helps to maintain confidence. It is too easy for sheriffs to become detached and suspect social workers' motives." (Sheriff)

It was also recognised, however, that liaison arrangements had the potential to diminish confidence in services as local liaison arrangements were considered to be an effective means of assessing the competence of particular social workers.
Although most sheriffs generally favoured the idea that the liaison could increase understanding of the social work perspective, more detailed analysis of specific responses indicates that many sheriffs considered good liaison to exist only when social workers adopted their perspectives.

There was consensus amongst interviewees that good liaison enhanced service performance. However, the examples given by interviewees often indicated that liaison is defined as good when sheriffs tell the social workers what they are to do with regard to service provision and the social workers comply with this.

PROCURATOR FISCAL RESPONSES TO LIAISON ARRANGEMENTS

Liaison Arrangements

The liaison arrangements between procurators fiscal and social workers are generally organised either around particular areas of service or around the prosecution of cases where a child is the victim, rather than the types of local or regional meetings which characterised liaison between sheriffs and social workers. Procurators fiscal generally liaise with their local area social work office through a nominated representative of the procurator fiscal service who co-ordinates contact with social workers. The exception was one interviewee who commented that they attended their local consultative committee at the Sheriff Court to which a social worker had recently been appointed.

Effectiveness of Liaison

General satisfaction was expressed with many aspects of liaison arrangements, aside from cases involving children, about which procurators fiscal had mixed views and this is discussed in more detail below. A common view was that liaison had enhanced the effectiveness of service provision in respect of breach.

Two difficulties had beset breach proceedings in the past: Firstly, social workers had often appeared unsure of the nature and extent of evidence required to prove a breach beyond reasonable doubt. Secondly, there were differences of view amongst procurators fiscal as to what comprised sufficiency of evidence.

In many areas the first difficulty had been addressed by procurators fiscal discussing with social workers the kinds of evidence required and going through breach reports indicating where improvement had to be made. With regard to the second difficulty, the nominated liaison officers within several procurator fiscal offices had played a key role in co-ordinating views on this matter and ensuring that a more uniform view was conveyed to social workers.

Liaison arrangements have led to greater procurator fiscal confidence in social work service and to shared understanding. An example of this was in the area where an experimental bail information scheme operated. Initially procurators fiscal had been sceptical about the scheme, considering it to be costly and disruptive. Regular meetings between social workers and the liaison officer within the procurator fiscal office had encouraged procurator fiscal staff to see the value of such schemes and the extent to which they save time and unnecessary disruption.

However, not all procurators fiscal defined effective liaison as shared understanding. As with sheriff interviewees, several procurators fiscal indicated that liaison was only effective when social workers complied with their requests. For example, one procurator fiscal described liaison over breach proceedings as effective because social workers had complied with procurator fiscal instructions. The same interviewee felt that liaison over (non-100 per cent funded) diversion schemes had been poor. They had wanted to widen the scope of an existing scheme. However, the social work authorities had been unable to do so because of lack of resources. In spite of procurators fiscal having information about resource constraint, this had not led to greater understanding on their part.

As highlighted above there were mixed views about the effectiveness of liaison arrangements in cases where a child was the victim. The responses indicate that there may be mutual suspicion between social workers and procurators fiscal in cases of child abuse. Interviewees generally felt that social workers were wary of passing information to procurators fiscal for fear that it would fall into police hands. The procurators fiscal also mistrusted social workers, as one interviewee commented:

"I do not want any cases to be jeopardised by the actions of social workers." (Procurator Fiscal)

There was consensus amongst procurators fiscal that through the provision of information, they could play an important role in assisting social workers to support child victims. The procurators fiscal also saw benefit in being able to turn to social workers for information instead of having to rely solely on police reports. A key issue was the need to develop a joint approach to individual cases and more effective liaison was considered to be the cornerstone of this.

Impact of National Objectives and Standards on Arrangements

A common perception was that the implementation of the National Objectives and Standards had made little or no impact on the nature and quality of liaison arrangements. Only one procurator fiscal commented that the standards had instigated major changes and also felt that social workers had adopted a more positive attitude towards procurator fiscal staff because of the regular contact. Social workers were making more attempts to liaise more regularly with procurators fiscal, meetings had become more formalised and arrangements had been enhanced by the availability of greater resources.

CONCLUSION

The impact of National Objectives and Standards implementation on liaison arrangements has been variable. In many areas the policy was perceived by interviewees to have had minimal impact, in others it was said to have led to formalisation of existing arrangements.

General satisfaction with arrangements was expressed by most procurators fiscal and sheriffs, although procurators fiscal had some concerns about liaison with social workers in cases where a child was the victim. Scottish Office officials, however, were less satisfied with the relationships between different groups within Central Government and considered that greater co-ordination was required between the social work and criminal justice policy administrators with regard to the future development of the policy.

An important issue to emerge from interviews has been the nature of effective liaison. Although this was generally defined as involving shared understandings or shared perspectives, in practice many interviewees believed that liaison was effective only where social workers complied with instructions and adopted the criminal justice point of view. Therefore it would appear that there were inequalities in the relationship between criminal justice agents and social workers. Criminal justice agents perceived themselves to be in a more powerful position and expected social workers to meet their requirements.

Successful implementation of the policy is dependent in part upon whether sentencers can be persuaded to consider the use of community based disposals more often and the policy expects liaison to play a key role in this. Given that the dialogue between sheriffs and social workers is not equally balanced, this may limit the degree to which liaison can function as a means of persuasion.

PART II

RESPONSES TO SERVICE PROVISION

CHAPTER FIVE

LOCAL AUTHORITY IMPLEMENTATION OF SERVICE STANDARDS

INTRODUCTION

As a result of National Objectives and Standards implementation, local authorities have to provide services which meet the national objectives, priorities and standards. Scottish Office officials were asked to comment on the progress that local authorities had made towards full implementation of the policy. Interviewees identified several facilitating and inhibiting factors. Key facilitators were linked to the nature and operation of the policy itself. Inhibitors were linked not only to perceived tensions within the policy but also to the wider context of policy implementation.

FACILITATORS

Three facilitators of standards implementation were identified by officials. These were: the protection of resources through the 100 per cent funding initiative; attempts to develop specialist services which were properly integrated into service delivery systems within social work departments as a whole; and the National Objectives and Standards framework itself which has provided clear objectives and priorities.

INHIBITORS

Service Level and Organisational Inhibitors

Scottish Office officials agreed that the local authorities had been slow to implement the policy initially but that it was now being progressed much more quickly[12].

It was believed that a contributory impediment to implementing the policy had been an unanticipated shortfall in local authority service levels at the point of policy implementation. There had been inaccurate information about the levels of service that local authorities had previously been providing. In the first stages therefore local authorities had to make up the shortfall in their services before they could progress further. It was estimated that this had delayed implementation by at least a year.

Organisational factors were also important and it was considered that the existing organisational structures in certain local authorities had inhibited implementation. Semi-specialist structures were singled out for particular criticism where they involved semi-specialists at the point of service delivery and generic managers who have wider concerns and priorities than solely offenders.

The professional view was that most of the required management structures were now in place although reorganisation was further advanced in some authorities, most notably the larger authorities:

> "In the time that they've had local authorities have achieved an encouraging amount. They all had a long way to go to get their own house in order. But they're now at the point where they can begin to address what they're in the business to do, that is to deliver quality services to the courts and offenders."(Professional)

Resource Inhibitors

Resource constraints were believed to have played a key role in the inhibition of policy implementation especially in the development of services focused on need. Key factors identified were: differing priorities within Central Government (discussed in Chapter Two); the policy context within which the National Objectives and Standards were being implemented; and the nature of the 100 per cent funding arrangements.

---

[12] The interviews with Scottish Office officials were conducted between November 1992 and January 1993.

Policy Context

Some concerns were expressed about the potential for the policy to be taken forward at the same time as other major social work initiatives such as community care. It was felt that in the competition for scarce resources, it could be difficult to maintain development of offender services consistent with the objectives of the policy:

> "Offender services are a small fish in a large pool. There is danger that the offender agenda will fall off the map or recede as other priorities come on stream. It's a very real problem and it has to be managed." (Professional)

The implication of this view will be considered in the next phase of the research.

100 per cent Funding and Service Development

The professional view identified several difficulties that arose from the 100 per cent funding arrangements. The 100 per cent funding created boundaries between offender services and other elements of local authority services which have an interest in the offender field, for example: mental health; addiction services; child and family care services. Greater scope existed for multi-service co-operation but this could be inhibited by the different arrangements for the funding of these services.

In addition, the policy requires local authorities to plan coherent strategies for the development of offender services as a totality and also to provide and manage these services economically, efficiently and effectively. The existing organisation of 100 per cent funding had led to a tension between these elements. This tension arose because central funding did not cover the full range of social work services in the criminal justice system. It was felt that local authorities would find it difficult to plan coherent strategies when different funding arrangements existed for various services. Unless 100 per cent funding was extended to all social work criminal justice services, it was believed that the policy might be less cost effective than otherwise.

Key Service Users

Sheriffs and procurators fiscal were asked about the quality and range of non-100 per cent services, for example, diversion from prosecution and social work services in respect of means enquiry and fines supervision. The majority of those interviewed agreed that non-100 per cent funded services were poorly developed in comparison with centrally funded services and that they were of low priority within social work departments.

In the case of fines supervision these factors were believed to have resulted in poor quality performance in what was otherwise perceived as a useful service. It was also recognised that resource constraints had inhibited the further development of diversion from prosecution schemes. Both sheriffs and procurators fiscal believed that diversion was a particularly effective way of dealing with certain categories of offender. Sheriffs commented that the courts were having to deal with too many mentally disordered offenders, minor breaches of the peace and minor drugs offences, which could be more appropriately dealt with outside the criminal justice system. A strong view was that diversion schemes should be placed within the scope of the 100 per cent funding initiative.

The Contribution of the Independent Sector: Inhibitors

The National Objectives and Standards state that local authorities should consider the contribution that the independent sector can make in the provision of services and resources for offenders. Officials agreed that local authorities had been slow to do so. Greater scope now existed for multi-agency collaboration in the development and delivery of offender services, although it was recognised that the quality of independent sector agencies was variable.

One of the key inhibitors of increased use of independent sector provision which was identified by interviewees, was that the local authorities had not yet uniformly developed the requisite skills in negotiation, contracting and monitoring to ensure that the purchaser/provider relationship between local authorities and independent agencies worked effectively.

In addition, it was believed that some local authority reluctance to make greater use of independent sector agencies reflected concerns that this was: "the thin end of the privatisation wedge". Officials commented that such concerns had been anticipated by Central Government and that an attempt had been made to allay anxieties by including in the funding initiative an arrangement whereby grant for criminal justice services was paid directly to local authorities. Where independent sector agencies were involved in service provision, the local authority had to fund them out of their grant. This ensured that the local authorities retained an element of control over their relationship with the independent sector.

CONCLUSION

There was consensus amongst interviewees that the local authorities had been slow to implement the policy initially but that it was now being taken forward at an increased pace. However, responses indicate that factors which were regarded by interviewees as facilitators of service provision, such as guaranteed funding for specified services, paradoxically may have played a part in inhibiting the policy from meeting some of its strategic objectives in the planning of services. Different funding arrangements for various services were believed to have impeded multi-service co-operation and made it difficult for local authorities to plan effectively.

Interviewees' responses indicate that the wider policy context within which the National Objectives and Standards are being implemented may have an impact on service development and on the future shape of the policy itself.

CHAPTER SIX
SOCIAL ENQUIRY REPORTS

INTRODUCTION

Social enquiry reports are one of the principal forms of communication between sheriffs and social workers. Although sheriffs are the main audience for the reports, procurators fiscal have access to them and on occasions read them to check the facts given in a report or make use of them as an independent source of information where there is a plea in mitigation. Although this use of social enquiry reports is ostensibly different from that of sheriffs, it was found in Chapter Three that many sheriffs use them for a similar purpose.

This chapter examines the extent to which National Objectives and Standards implementation are perceived to have had an impact on the content and presentation of social enquiry reports and on their efficiency and effectiveness as a medium of communication. Shrieval and procurator fiscal responses are discussed.

IMPACT OF NATIONAL OBJECTIVES AND STANDARDS

Many sheriffs and procurators fiscal interviewed said that there had been major improvements in social enquiry reports in recent years. There had been an increase in uniformity in presentation of the reports and better quality content. In addition to this, attention had been paid in reports to detailed discussion of the various disposals and the suitability of each for offenders; more information was being given about the aims of social work supervision and the goals that had to be achieved. These interviewees saw poor quality reports (defined as those containing inadequate recommendations) as being unusual and a result of immaturity or inexperience of individual social workers, rather than a reflection of the standard of reports generally. Most of these interviewees attributed the improvements directly to National Objectives and Standards implementation, though some of them saw improvement as being the result of more gradual changes over the last ten or so years. Factors involved in this were described as being the improved training and the greater "social responsibility" or "realism" of social workers, since more appeared now to accept that the gravity of certain offences merited custody. Interviewees who considered that social enquiry reports had improved in the last few years attributed this to good liaison between social workers and sheriffs. In some areas sheriffs had discussed the contents of social enquiry reports with social workers and indicated the factors which would carry weight with them. In one particular area the regional consultative committee had spent some time discussing the style of social enquiry reports and sheriffs had put forward suggestions for change. These suggestions had now been put into practice by social workers.

Aside from one sheriff interviewee (who commented that social enquiry reports had always been of high quality and therefore the National Objectives and Standards had had minimal impact), the view that National Objectives and Standards had little or no impact was more likely to be given by the minority of interviewees with negative views of social enquiry reports. Such interviewees tended to see social workers as "naive and gullible", accepting what the offender told them at face value, and that this was often at variance with the facts of the case. As a consequence these interviewees saw most of the recommendations made by social workers in their reports as being unrealistic:

> "Some conclusions leave a lot to be desired - they are sometimes ludicrously inadequate and inappropriate." (Sheriff)

The amount of detail in the reports also came in for criticism. Some of the information in the reports was felt to be irrelevant, in particular the "ancient history of the accused" or "a potted history of childhood diseases". Some reports were criticised as being repetitive, especially the information contained in the sections about educational and family background. The responses indicate that a more concise and streamlined report would find favour with these sheriffs and procurators fiscal.

SERVICE DELIVERY

The National Objectives and Standards state that social enquiry reports must be complete within the 21 day period allowed by statute or within 14 days if an offender is in custody. Most sheriffs and procurators fiscal commented that reports were delivered within these timescales although there was one area where around 25 per cent of reports were usually late. Nevertheless many sheriffs received reports on the day of the court rather than on the preceding day, as stipulated in the National Objectives and Standards. This caused difficulty if there was a busy court and in particular for the remand court. Sheriffs often had to read 20 or 30 reports. This imposed limits on the extent to which they could assimilate the details and most said that they tended to skim reports concentrating on the conclusions and recommendations.

ORAL AND STAND DOWN REPORTS

Given the time and resources that are required to write social enquiry reports, sheriffs were asked whether there were any types of cases for which they could as easily be served by oral or stand-down reports. The majority of sheriffs felt that there were very few situations where it would be safe to rely on these kinds of reports. A need for the in-depth and objective assessment provided by the social enquiry report was stressed. One sheriff commented that they were against oral reports as a matter of principle. Full consideration had to be given to all the relevant information, especially if someone was at risk of custody. Only one sheriff felt that in most cases oral reports could be used instead of social enquiry reports, particularly in those cases where custody was a foregone conclusion. This interviewee was highly dissatisfied with the social enquiry reports which they currently received

CONCLUSION

Most sheriffs and procurators fiscal felt that the National Objectives and Standards had made a major impact on the quality and presentation of the reports. Only a minority of interviewees felt that the National Objectives and Standards had had minimal impact and were dissatisfied with service provision. However, even those who viewed social enquiry reports positively, felt that improvements to the service could be made by ensuring that the reports were available the day before the court. Concerns were also expressed as to the level of detail in the report, although some sheriffs saw the main advantage of the social enquiry report as compared with other reports to be the in-depth analysis that it contained.

CHAPTER SEVEN
COMMUNITY BASED DISPOSALS

INTRODUCTION

The policy objective of promoting and enhancing the range and quality of community based social work disposals available to the courts involves a requirement that social work departments ensure that services are managed and supervised in such a manner that they have the confidence of the courts. Sheriffs were asked to comment on the range, quality and effectiveness of probation orders; community service schemes and services targeted on young adult offenders. Procurators fiscal were asked to comment on the efficiency and effectiveness of breach procedures in both probation and community service.

PROBATION

Probation was viewed by most sheriffs as a rehabilitative and reformative disposal suitable only for offenders who had significant personal or social problems which contributed to their offending behaviour. There was general agreement amongst sheriff interviewees that probation services were operating satisfactorily. Nevertheless, there was variation in views about the extent to which National Objectives and Standards implementation has had an impact on service provision. In some areas substantial improvements in services were said to have occurred, in others a pattern of gradual change over a number of years preceding the implementation of the standards was discernible.

Major Change

In the areas where there had been substantial improvements in services, interviewees identified four key changes which had occurred as a direct result of standards implementation. Firstly, sheriffs had more information about the content of probation supervision. The main source of this information was social enquiry reports. Secondly, sheriffs were now more confident that there were better levels of supervision, partly as a result of receiving regular feedback from supervising officers on the progress and outcome of probation orders. Thirdly, there was a greater number of probation services available, for example specialist counselling programmes and intensive supervision. Fourthly, sheriffs felt that services were better resourced.

Gradual Change

Several interviewees had noticed a gradual improvement in service provision. In some areas this had taken place within the last four years, in others improvements had taken place over a longer period. A common view was that probation had fallen into disrepute in the mid-seventies following changes instigated by the 1968 Social Work (Scotland) Act when social workers replaced probation officers in the administration and delivery of probation services. Probation supervision was perceived to have been lax or in some cases non-existent. A gradual improvement was perceived to have begun in the late seventies and early eighties and was attributed by most of this group of interviewees to a shift from genericism to specialism amongst some social work practitioners. The key elements of probation practice that had changed were, that there was now more rigorous enforcement of breach procedures and again better feedback from social workers on the outcome of supervision. Although these changes had occurred well before the introduction of the National Objectives and Standards it was generally felt that the implementation of the policy had speeded up the process of change. Two important factors contributing to this were the increased availability of social work resources for probation through the 100 per cent funding arrangement and organisational changes within the authorities.

Service Development

Although the quality and range of service was regarded as high, interviewees nevertheless thought that there was considerable scope for broadening the range of probation services available. High tariff probation schemes were viewed favourably by most sheriffs and it was felt that these schemes should be more widely available. In areas where high tariff probation existed, concerns were expressed about the patchy provision of placements on some of the schemes. Whilst recognising that these schemes were resource intensive, sheriffs nevertheless felt that high tariff probation was one of the most effective community based disposals as it combined a high level of control with intensive supervision and counselling. As a consequence they considered that the service more useful and justified the costs.

COMMUNITY SERVICE

Most interviewees' perception was that the policy had had little impact on community service schemes. The National Objectives and Standards for the operation of community service in Scotland were published on 1 April 1989. This element of the policy had therefore been in place for a longer period than other areas of service provision. As a consequence, it might be expected that arrangements for the delivery of community service schemes would be better developed than other aspects of the policy.

Impact of National Objectives and Standards Implementation

Sheriffs were asked whether they considered that the implementation of the National Objectives and Standards and the 100 per cent funding arrangements had had an impact on the nature and level of service provision. The majority of interviewees commented that community service was good in their area and this had increased their confidence in community service.

Resource Issues

Concerns about the resourcing of service provision were expressed by a number of sheriffs, including some of those who were generally satisfied with the operation of community service. In several areas schemes occasionally came under pressure of numbers. Under these circumstances sheriffs said they had sometimes been asked by the social work department if they would consider custody or a less "serious" alternative instead of community service. Some sheriffs believed that community service had become a victim of its own success. Because sheriffs had more confidence in community service they were using it for greater numbers of offenders and this had caused a strain on services. This contrasts with their views on sentencing aims and decisions, discussed in Chapter Three, where sheriffs' responses indicated that confidence in a disposal did not guarantee that it would be used more frequently.

Quality and Range of Service Provision

The majority of sheriffs interviewed expressed a high degree of satisfaction with community service in their areas. The high quality of service was attributed to the rigorous monitoring of schemes undertaken by social workers, the level of supervision and the degree of feedback that was provided to the courts. In particular, where sheriffs felt that breach procedures operated well, this enhanced the credibility of community service as an alternative to custody and increased their confidence in it. One sheriff commented that community service had been the single most important development in recent years, describing it as being "properly punitive" and yet giving offenders a sense of self respect and a degree of satisfaction. Quality of service provision was only specifically associated in a few areas with the implementation of the National Objectives and Standards. Sheriffs felt less able to comment on the range of schemes available as they receive very little information about them, other than that in social enquiry reports. However, lack of information about the content of schemes was not seen as being problematic as they had a high level of confidence in community service staff.

A minority of sheriffs commented that they were extremely dissatisfied with the way in which community service operated. Problems identified were the length of time it took for community service to be put into operation and inadequacies in following breach procedures. In the absence of further information about schemes, dissatisfaction in these respects tended to generate anxiety that the schemes were "sloppily supervised". These sheriffs believed that the public perceived community service to be a soft option with the schemes having little if any impact on offending behaviour. Several sheriffs had become increasingly disenchanted with the numbers of young offenders who continued to return to court having been given the maximum number of hours. Sheriffs with these views felt that young offenders did not perceive community service to be a punishment. A strong view was that the schemes should involve a greater degree of work and effort on the part of the offender.

Assessment Procedures

Concerns were expressed by several interviewees about the adequacy of procedures for assessing the suitability of an offender for community service. As a result of the implementation of the National Objectives and Standards, community service assessments were undertaken by social workers. Sheriffs no longer received a separate report from the community service officer. The majority of sheriffs interviewed felt that this was unsatisfactory. Assessments were believed to have been more balanced and realistic in the past when they had been undertaken by the community service workers who operated the schemes.

Concerns were also expressed about the numbers of orders that were not fulfilled on health grounds. More careful screening of offenders during assessment for community service was suggested.

Policy and Service Development

Although most sheriffs were satisfied with community service provision, they nevertheless held strong views as to how the service could be further developed. Most interviewees felt that the scope of community service could be extended but contradictory views were expressed as to how this could be achieved.

The majority of sheriffs were strongly of the view that the criteria for the use of community service should be relaxed. It was felt that community service would be a useful alternative to a financial penalty for those on social security or low income. In addition, the discipline and effort involved in a community service order would be of benefit to less serious categories of offenders, especially if they were unemployed. A common view was that sheriffs already use community service either as a sentence "in its own right" or as an alternative to a financial penalty:

> "I suspect sheriffs impose community service orders knowing full well that they would not send them into custody but think that community service is right for them." (Sheriff)

However, a minority of sheriffs believed that relaxed criteria would devalue the community service order as an alternative to custody. One view was that the maximum number of community service hours should be extended from 240 to 500. Sheriffs considered that the extension of hours would enhance the standing of community service as an alternative to custody and increase the public's confidence in it.

BREACH OF PROBATION AND COMMUNITY SERVICE ORDERS

The National Objectives and Standards set out service standards and detailed guidelines for breach procedures. The standards state that social workers and procurators fiscal must set up local liaison arrangements to expedite applications for breach. Procurator fiscal views were sought on the effectiveness and efficiency of breach proceedings in their area.

Procurators fiscal generally had mixed views about the operation of breach procedures. In some areas they considered that breach procedures worked well and that the quality of breach reports was high.

However, strong concerns were expressed by other procurators fiscal about the effectiveness of breach procedures. One view was that social workers did not appear to understand that a contested breach had to be proved beyond reasonable doubt. Because they have access to police reports in such cases, procurators fiscal found it easier to progress probation breaches involving commission of further offences than breaches of other conditions. Social workers were often unfamiliar with the standard of evidence required to prove a breach. Particular difficulties had occurred in respect of probation where, unlike community service, the breach had to be corroborated[13]. Procurators fiscal sometimes received "bland" statements in breach reports rather than the detailed case histories which were required. The reports often included the names of several social workers and it was not made clear what the involvement of each was in the case.

The National Objectives and Standards give detailed guidance on the requirements for breach procedures for both community service and probation. However, procurator fiscal responses suggested that the policy has had minimal impact on efficiency and effectiveness of breach procedures in many areas. Effective implementation would have removed the apparent lack of knowledge or understanding about the requirement of breach on the part of some social workers. Any improvement in quality of breach reports was attributed by procurators fiscal to improved liaison (Chapter Four).

Phase Two of the research programme will examine the efficiency and effectiveness of breach procedures in relation to probation. This will include consideration of the role of procurators fiscal, social workers and other agencies involved in breach procedures.

SERVICES FOR YOUNG ADULT OFFENDERS

One of the aims of the policy is to target community based disposals on young adults at risk of repeat offending. Sheriffs were asked to comment on the range, quality and effectiveness of services that had been developed.

---

[13] The standard of proof for breach of probation has changed as a result of the implementation of the Prisoners and Criminal Proceedings (Scotland) Act 1993. Schedule 5, paragraph 7 provides that the evidence of one witness shall be sufficient to establish a failure to comply with any requirement of the order.

Impact of National Objectives and Standards Implementation

The National Objectives and Standards were not perceived to have had a major impact on the development of new services nor on the performance of schemes already in existence. Only one sheriff identified National Objectives and Standards implementation as providing the impetus behind the intensive probation scheme that had been initiated in their area. This sheriff considered that the reorganisation of the local social work department had played a major role in facilitating the development of specialist schemes.

Range of Services

Shrieval responses indicated that a wide range of services have been developed but that service provision was rather patchy. The range of schemes developed by social work departments included intensive probation schemes, specialist alcohol and drug programmes and accommodation schemes. Schemes had also been developed by independent sector agencies, for example, a National Children's Homes alternative to custody scheme. Where no schemes for young adult offenders were available, sheriffs were keen to see the development of programmes tailored to their specific needs.

Effectiveness of Service

Sheriffs had mixed views about the effectiveness of specialist services for young adult offenders. Specialist schemes were thought unlikely to be effective given the intractable nature of the people with whom they had to work. However, sheriffs had a high regard for intensive probation schemes because, in addition to help, there was a large element of control in the supervision of the offenders.

Service Development

Concerns were expressed that insufficient attention had been paid by local authorities to the development of specialist schemes for young adults involved in less serious offences:

> "The scheme for young adult offenders in my area only operates as an alternative to custody. An effective scheme for those who offend less seriously would nip the pattern of offending in the bud." (Sheriff)

If it was possible to relax the custody criteria for the use of community service, a common view was that community service would be a particularly useful disposal for this group of young offenders as the work placements would instil a sense of self respect and discipline them.

CONCLUSION

There was variation in the views expressed by sheriffs and procurators fiscal on the impact of National Objectives and Standards implementation on the range and quality of community based disposals. Shrieval responses indicated that the policy may be seen to have had a positive impact on probation where it appears to have led to major improvement in services in certain areas.

Probation services were highly regarded by most interviewees but were viewed as being suitable for a limited number of offenders. Two factors which contributed to quality of service were identified as increased specialisation on the part of social workers, and more rigorous supervision of orders. This last was thought to enhance the control element of probation. In some areas National Objectives and Standards were perceived to have paved the way for major changes in the quality and range of probation services, in others to have increased the pace of change.

Specialist schemes for young adult offenders were perceived to have been minimally affected by National Objectives and Standards implementation. Sheriffs were sceptical about the effectiveness of specialist schemes for this group although intensive probation was viewed favourably. Most schemes were targeted on high risk young offenders and it was felt that greater concentration on less serious offenders might be an effective way of reducing the incidence of crime amongst this age group.[14]

---

[14] The suggestions made by sheriffs as to how community service and services for young adult offenders could be developed would require amending legislation.

CHAPTER EIGHT
THROUGHCARE

INTRODUCTION

Throughcare is the service provided by social work and other associated agencies to prisoners and their families from the point of sentence or remand, during imprisonment and following release into the community. Because throughcare is the responsibility of both the Scottish Prison Service and local authorities, building up an effective service requires good inter-agency co-operation.

Throughcare was identified by Scottish Office officials in social work and criminal justice as being particularly poorly developed. Several factors contributed to this. In the development of the objectives and standards it was felt there had been a preoccupation with the courts and the judiciary in an attempt to increase the availability and use of alternatives to custody. In addition to this, community based throughcare services had been the least well developed service prior to policy implementation and therefore had the most progress to make to meet the required standards.

This chapter will examine Parole Board and parole administrator views on the quality and effectiveness of throughcare services in respect of report writing, social work services in prison and community based supervision.

HOME CIRCUMSTANCES REPORTS

One of the key concerns of the Parole Board is how offenders are going to respond once they are returned to the community. Home circumstances reports have an important contribution to make to Parole Board decision making in this matter.

There were mixed views about the quality of home circumstances reports and the degree of impact that National Objectives and Standards implementation may have had. One view was that the policy had made an impact on the quality of content and presentation of the report. The reports now indicated that social workers had undertaken a more detailed examination of the home background of offenders and their families. There was now more information about the community services available to support the offender on release and now social workers enquired into the attitudes of other people in the community towards specific offenders. This was felt to be of particular importance in the case of sex offenders. The reports also indicated that social workers had searched social work records, where appropriate, to see how an offender had responded to earlier social work intervention.

Another view, however, was that there had been no improvement in reports. The quality of report was linked to the experience and capability of the individual social worker. On occasions reports were still received that were based on one meeting with the offender's family and none with the offender. It was also felt that information in reports was often not fully checked. Report writers appeared to take the offender's views at face value rather than checking out the facts, especially in respect of job offers, which might turn out to be fictitious.

It is difficult to draw conclusions from these contradictory views. Throughcare objectives and standards are in the early stages of implementation and it may be that there has been insufficient time for improvement to filter through in a consistent way. This issue will need to be further explored in the next phase of the evaluation.

PRISON BASED SOCIAL WORK REPORTS

The assessment of risk is one of the most important factors governing Parole Board decisions and prison based social work reports have an important role to play in the measurement of risk. The reports should give details of any "release package" which the prison based social worker has prepared. Parole Board members expect these reports to indicate whether the prisoner has taken steps to address their offending behaviour by, for example, attending counselling sessions, especially in the case of sex offenders and prisoners with alcohol problems.

The quality of report writing was generally felt to be variable. The implementation of the National Objectives and Standards was perceived to have had only a limited impact to date.

As in home circumstances reports, there were comments that social workers relied too much on what they had been told by the prisoners without checking it against other sources of information. On occasion reports seemed to be based on a limited knowledge of the offender and sometimes gave wrong information.

However, interviewees thought that one encouraging feature was the increased level of liaison between prison and community based social workers. This was particularly helpful in assessing risk. In sex offender cases information from the family, the local community and, where appropriate, the victim now appeared more frequently in prison social workers' reports.

Interviewees generally considered that improvements in report writing were likely to be gradual because of the need for greater training on the part of the social workers and the need for more time to develop their skills.

SOCIAL WORK SERVICES IN PRISONS

Social work services in prisons are not (at the time of writing) subject to National Standards. However detailed guidance on policy and practice has been issued in the document *Continuity Through Co-operation*. This document describes the main activities of prison based social workers as: the assessment of personal and social need; individual and group work with prisoners and their families to assist with eventual resettlement into the community; and the development and provision of programmes of intervention to address problems commonly presented by prisoners. It also states that social workers must be "freed to undertake professional tasks" and that the development of the prison officer's welfare role has a key role to play in this[15]. Interviewees were asked to comment on the impact of *Continuity Through Co-operation* on the quality and range of social work services in prisons.

One of the main changes noted was that there had been increased levels of co-operation between social workers and other agencies, especially psychiatric services. Several joint projects had been established. However, changes were sporadic and, in some prisons, co-operation between social workers and other agencies was minimal. One example given was a prison where there were two programmes for prisoners with alcohol problems, one run by social workers, the other by an independent sector agency. There was no indication reported of communication between the social workers and the independent agency, even although they both offered the same service.

Parole Board members were keen to see further development of collaborative projects, as inter-disciplinary approaches were considered to be the most effective way of dealing with difficult prisoners.

A more recent change in one prison unit, noted by an interviewee, was that social workers now attended meetings between the Parole Board and prison staff during Parole Board visits to the prison. This interviewee commented that formerly only prison staff who happened to be on duty at the time attended these meetings and this did not always include staff who were involved in parole matters. Social work participation was thought to be particularly helpful when discussing individual prisoners because social workers were able to provide a different perspective from that of prison officers:

> "Social workers sat in on the meeting and the meeting was much better for that reason. We got into areas of discussion that normally we hadn't got into before so that was a plus. If that's happening across the board then its a big plus." (Parole Board Member)

Effectiveness

Opinions varied about the effectiveness of prison-based social work. One view was that specialist services which had been developed by social workers were particularly effective, especially programmes for sex offenders. However, this view was not shared by all interviewees. Concerns were expressed about the low level of places and this had made social work services less effective than they might otherwise have been.

There was, however, consensus amongst interviewees that prison based social workers' reports often suggested that social work contact with the prisoner had been minimal. In some cases the interview between prisoner and social worker for the purpose of writing the report was felt to have been the only contact.

> "When we are visiting prisons and we speak to prisoners about the prison based social workers, they sometimes say they don't even know that there is one there. I think that there needs to be a lot of work done internally on that basis." (Parole Board Member)

In their view, the lack of contact indicated that social workers had little opportunity to help prisoners address their offending behaviour and this led to some doubts about the effectiveness of the social worker role. A key

---

[15] SPS/SWSG (1989) *Continuity Through Co-operation: A National Framework of Policy and Practice Guidance for Social Work in Scottish Penal Establishments:* Paragraphs 3.42 and 3.43.

concern was that prisoners' problems were often not identified until the point when parole was being considered. It was felt that intervention at a much earlier stage would be more effective. One consequence of this was that Parole Board decisions on a particular case had often been delayed. Interviewees believed that time and resource constraints had been the main causes of these problems.

A parole administrator suggested that more effective use of sentence planning would resolve these difficulties for certain categories of prisoners. Sentence planning is intended to enable prisoners to address their problems and to provide opportunities for personal development. A parole administrator commented however that the current operation of sentence planning was inadequate. It was described as a "passive process" where prisoners were "sentence planned" as part of other general induction procedures. They believed that the plans were rarely put into operation. It was felt that more effective planning could identify prisoners' problems and develop action programmes in order to address them.

SUPERVISION IN THE COMMUNITY

Information about Service Provision

The community based social worker's report was the main source of information that the Parole Board members had about available service provision. They did not consider this to be sufficient and felt that there needed to be more liaison between social work policy advisers, professionals and the Parole Board in order to help them identify suitable services. Parole Board interviewees did not have enough information about the 100 per cent funding initiative and programmes that may have been developed as a consequence of the throughcare objectives and standards implementation. Much of the Parole Board's contact with social work administrators and professionals was through circulars rather than face to face contact. Board members were keen to have more regular meetings as greater knowledge about services was linked to improved quality of decision making.

Range, Content and Effectiveness of Supervision

Interviewees had mixed views about the range and quality of community social work supervision. One view was that the range of service provision was gradually improving, particularly in respect of accommodation. A key issue however was the need for greater co-operation to develop joint programmes between social workers and specialist agencies. If joint programmes were more widely available, interviewees felt that this would enable the Parole Board to recommend the earlier release of certain categories of offender, especially sex offenders and prisoners who had psychiatric problems. Well developed rehabilitation programmes were also regarded as essential for young offenders, although the numbers of young offenders released on statutory supervision were small. Mixed views were expressed about the role of the independent sector in the provision of services in the community. Some interviewees felt that collaboration was extremely effective and that independent sector agencies were the most innovative in developing services. Ex-prisoners were believed to respond better to independent sector programmes because they did not appear to be "authority based". Others, however, considered that the independent sector only had a minor role to play and that local authority social work input was more important.

The supervision reports that were received indicated that the nature of supervision was also improving in some cases as social workers appeared to have greater knowledge about their clients. However, these improvements were patchy. In some instances there was evidence that there had been no supervision and officials commented that reports from supervising officers were often not submitted as frequently as they should have been, especially in the case of life licencees. Interviewees stated that one common feature of the supervision of this group was that where the Parole Board requested quarterly reports, social workers apparently believed that they only had to have contact with the offender on a quarterly basis. The expectations of the Board were, however, that these offenders would be seen much more frequently. A further concern of interviewees was that additional conditions that were attached to many licences were often not supervised adequately. It was felt that lack of resources and time often contributed to this.

IMPACT OF THE IMPLEMENTATION OF NATIONAL OBJECTIVES AND STANDARDS

Interviewees were less clear about the impact of National Objectives and Standards implementation on services. It was felt that the policy was still in the early stage of implementation - indeed one interviewee identified a social work authority where the standards had not been implemented as yet. A strong view was that the quality of supervision was linked more to the abilities and commitment of individual social workers and this was felt to be variable. Some interviewees commented that social work supervision required a better balance of control and help:

"From my experience the help element is the priority with individual social workers..." (Parole Administrator)

Concerns were expressed that a greater element of control would be required when the Prisoners and Criminal Proceedings (Scotland) Act 1993 was implemented. This would result in the possibility that offenders serving between 12 months to four years and who were considered to be a high risk to the public, could have a supervised release order imposed on them at the point of sentence. These offenders would be "conscripts to supervision". Concerns were expressed by the parole administrator about the ability of social workers to deal effectively with such offenders. Increased training for social workers and higher levels of resources were felt to be necessary.

CONCLUSION

Throughcare services were perceived to be the most poorly developed element of social work criminal justice services prior to National Objectives and Standards implementation and thus far the policy appears to have had only limited impact. However, interviewee responses indicate that improvements in services are beginning to appear. For example, in some areas there have been enhanced levels of inter-agency co-operation and there have been occasional examples of better quality report writing. Nevertheless interviewees held contradictory views on these issues and this would suggest that National Objectives and Standards implementation has yet[16] to filter through in a consistent manner.

---

[16] This report was written in 1993.

CHAPTER NINE
CONCLUSION

PERCEIVED EFFECTIVENESS OF POLICY IMPLEMENTATION

Services

Interviewee responses indicate that the quality of service provision throughout Scotland may be uneven and that within individual social work authorities some services appear better developed than others. This pattern is also reflected in the impact that the implementation of the National Objectives and Standards may have made on the quality and range of particular social work services.

Services where the policy is perceived to have led to major improvements were identified by interviewees as the provision of social enquiry reports and probation but these improvements had not occurred in all social work authorities. The impact on throughcare is perceived to have been more limited. Throughcare services were considered to have been the least well developed aspect of social work criminal justice services. The apparently limited impact of policy implementation may be due to the amount of ground that this service has to make up to reach the quality and range of service required by the standards.

The next phase of the evaluation examines the extent to which local factors affecting particular services may account for the differences in levels of impact and the extent to which perceptions of impact are borne out in practice.

Liaison

The implementation of the policy was perceived to have had limited impact on the nature of liaison arrangements that exist between procurators fiscal, sheriffs and social workers, other than to formalise those arrangements which already existed. However, implementation was considered to have given the issue of alternatives to custody for high risk offenders an increased prominence in discussion. Phase Two of the research programme will consider social work practitioners' and managers' responses to liaison arrangements.

Perceptions of the effectiveness of liaison arrangements within Central Government and between Central Government and other agencies were mixed. Increased collaboration between criminal justice and social work administrators and professionals may be necessary to facilitate future policy development and to promote a co-ordinated criminal justice policy in relation to criminal justice services within Central Government.

KEY FACILITATORS AND INHIBITORS OF POLICY IMPLEMENTATION

The protection of resources through the 100 per cent funding initiative and the framework of the National Objectives and Standards, which provides clear objectives and priorities, are key facilitators of policy implementation.
Paradoxically these facilitators appear to have inhibited certain aspects of policy implementation. In particular, a view was that unless 100 per cent funding was extended to all elements of social work criminal justice services it would be difficult for local authorities to develop coherent strategies and provide a cost-effective service. Areas of service not covered by central funding were perceived by sentencers to be under-resourced and of low priority in social work authorities.

Tensions that had arisen over the financing of services and the development of the monitoring system may have contributed to difficulties in the development of management information systems. Different responsibilities in relation to policy implementation explain variations in priority to which officials assign particular elements of the policy. These variations reflect the potential for conflict within the policy itself between the framework of the objectives and standards and the elements of the policy which highlight the need to develop services within available resources.

Local authorities were initially slow to implement the policy. A key explanation of this was felt to be the organisational structures of local authorities which existed at the time new arrangements were being introduced. However, the policy requires local authorities to develop organisational and management structures geared to coherent service delivery before they can deliver the services to the requirement of the Standards. This has taken time and may account for the delays. Local government reform which is planned for 1996 will impact further on delays in the development of these structures.

Independent sector involvement in the provision of services was felt to have been inhibited in part by local authority fears about privatisation, inadequacies in local authorities' ability to ensure that the purchaser/provider relationship worked effectively, and the variable quality of independent sector services.

IMPACT OF ARRANGEMENTS FOR POLICY IMPLEMENTATION ON SENTENCING

The success of the policy in achieving a reduction in custody will depend, in part, on sentencers being willing to make greater use of community based disposals for high risk categories of offenders. Shrieval responses indicate that it may be difficult for the National Objectives and Standards to have an impact on sentencing. Although sheriffs endorsed the main aims of the policy, they were reluctant to identify themselves as adopting a particular theoretical perspective on sentencing. It was found that shrieval views on the sentencing of offenders at high risk of custody, a key target, appears primarily to be informed by their beliefs about public interest and expectations rather than their understanding of what social work services could provide. Under these circumstances liaison arrangements between sheriffs and social workers are, in themselves, unlikely to effect a change in shrieval perspectives. Sheriffs have clear expectations about the contribution which social workers can make to criminal justice services. They viewed liaison as a vehicle for communicating their expectations rather than as a means of exchanging views between equals. Any attempt by social workers to effect a change in these expectations will be made more difficult by the perceived inequalities inherent in the relationship between social work and criminal justice.

Key issues for the next phase of the evaluation are: to consider in more detail factors which might have a role in shaping shrieval perspectives; and the apparent divergence in their views about the impact of enhanced confidence in disposals on sentencing decisions.

ANNEX 1

THE HISTORY AND DEVELOPMENT OF THE NATIONAL STANDARDS AND THE 100 PER CENT FUNDING INITIATIVE

The full history of the development of the National Objectives and Standards and the 100 per cent funding initiative has yet to be written. However this annex, which was written on the basis of Central Government documents, outlines briefly the background to the development of the policy.

Under arrangements introduced by the Social Work (Scotland) Act 1968, local authorities paid for the majority of social work services in the criminal justice system out of their general income. The 1968 Act transferred all of the statutory functions of the probation service to local authorities and social workers became responsible for supervising probationers. Probation and other local authority funded criminal justice services were therefore in competition for resources with other areas of social work provision.

One exception to the general funding arrangements was prison based social work. Responsibility for the provision of this service was transferred from the Scottish Home and Health Department (SHHD) to local authorities in 1973 although it continued to be funded by Central Government. It was intended that prison social work should become part of a broader throughcare strategy developed by local authorities. However, this depended on co-operation between social work and prison managers and this was slow to develop. A formal review of social work in the Scottish penal system was undertaken in 1985 by Professor Parsloe on behalf of Her Majesty's Chief Inspector of Prisons. This review recommended that a national framework for prison social work should be established. Accordingly a drafting group was set up comprising representatives from Social Work Services Group (SWSG) and Prison Group (SHHD) and the local authorities. In 1989 Central Government published *Continuity Through Co-operation*[17], a framework for policy and practice guidance for prison based social work services.

Community Service (CS) was introduced in Scotland in 1977 and in its early stages of development was funded by Central Government. Initially it was only available as part of a probation order. As a result of the Community Service by Offenders (Scotland) Act 1978, courts were able to make community service orders from 40 to a maximum of 240 hours and also to continue using them as part of a probation order. Schemes were to be 80 per cent funded by Central Government for the first five years of operation, 70 per cent for the next five years and 100 per cent funded by the local authorities thereafter. Operational guidelines were published by SWSG in 1980.

Considerable tension built up between local authorities and Central Government in the early 1980s over the funding of community service. The local authorities wanted Central Government funding to continue after the initial ten years of schemes. Agreement was reached to continue the current funding arrangements on the understanding that a joint review of the range of social work criminal justice services would be undertaken.

In 1983 the Joint Review Group on Services to Offenders was set up. The group comprised representatives from The Scottish Office and local authorities. However, discussions on improvements to offender services foundered on the issue of funding and the Group became caught up in the wider tensions about public expenditure between Central Government and the local authorities.

A survey by the policy sub-group of the Scottish Community Service Group[18] (SCSG) in 1985 highlighted variations in practice in community service schemes and geographical unevenness of provision. Rationing of services had also occurred in some areas and lack of resources in others had resulted in the temporary closure of schemes. Pressure grew from local authorities, the judiciary and groups such as SCSG for the development of National Standards to ensure evenness of provision across Scotland and for guaranteed funding.

In December 1987 the Scottish Office announced that 100 per cent Central Government funding of community service would commence on 1 April 1989. A consultation group was set up of representatives from: The Scottish Office; Association of Directors of Social Work (ADSW); Convention of Scottish Local Authorities (COSLA); Crown Office; Sheriffs' Association; District Courts Administration. This group was to develop National Objectives and Standards for community service.

During this period the prison population continued to rise, overcrowding intensified and there was a spate of prison disturbances. The Secretary of State for Scotland in a speech to the Howard League for Penal Reform in 1988, said that prison was not the ideal environment in which to reform and rehabilitate offenders (although prison was still considered to be appropriate for the most serious categories of offenders). The overall

---

[17] SPS/SWSG (1989) *Continuity Through Co-operation: A National Framework of Policy and Practice Guidance for Social Work in Scottish Penal Establishments.* The Scottish Prison Service/Social Work Services Group.

[18] The Scottish Community Service Group represents community service schemes throughout Scotland.

aim of Central Government was therefore to create a situation where prison would be used as sparingly as possible. It was believed that this could be achieved by improving the quality and increasing the quantity of community based disposals and improving the quality of statutory supervision of released prisoners. While arrangements were in hand to ensure the quality and quantity of community service schemes, there was a concern to bring other core social work criminal justice services in line with CS, in particular those services which used the bulk of local authority expenditure (probation, social enquiry reports and related services, and community based throughcare services). With this in mind a consultation group was set up in 1989 to review social work criminal justice services. This group comprised representatives from: Scottish Office; the judiciary, including the Sheriffs' Association; COSLA; ADSW; British Association of Social Workers; Scottish Association for the Care and Resettlement of Offenders; Association of Chief Police Officers (Scotland). Separate sub-groups were set up to review finance, throughcare services, probation and court services, and to develop National Objectives and Standards.

The National Objectives and Standards for social work services in the criminal justice system and the 100 per cent Central Government funding arrangements were implemented from 1991. The 100 per cent funding does not extend to all social work criminal justice services. Central Government has made a commitment in principle to extend the funding to include diversion from prosecution, deferred sentence supervision; fines supervision, and means enquiry. However, at the time of writing (1993) these services continue to be funded by local authorities.

REFERENCES

Brown, L., Levy, L. and McIvor, G. (1998) *Social Work and Criminal Justice: The National and Local Context.* Edinburgh: The Stationery Office.

Brown, L. and Levy, L. (1998) *Social Work and Criminal Justice: Sentencer Decision Making.* Edinburgh: The Stationery Office.

McAra, L. (1998) *Social Work and Criminal Justice: Early Arrangements.* Edinburgh: The Stationery Office.

McAra, L. (1998a) *Social Work and Criminal Justice: Parole Board Decision Making.* Edinburgh: The Stationery Office.

McIvor, G. and Barry, M. (1998) *Social Work and Criminal Justice: Probation.* Edinburgh: The Stationery Office.

McIvor, G. and Barry, M. (1998a) *Social Work and Criminal Justice: Community Based Throughcare.* Edinburgh: The Stationery Office.

Paterson, F. and Tombs, J. (1998) *Social Work and Criminal Justice: The Impact of Policy.* Edinburgh: The Stationery Office.

Social Work Services Group (1991) *National Objectives and Standards for Social Work Services in the Criminal Justice System.* Edinburgh: The Scottish Office.

SPS/SWSG (1989) *Continuity Through Co-operation: A National Framework of Policy and Practice Guidelines for Social Work in Scottish Penal Establishments.* Edinburgh: The Scottish Prison Service/Social Work Services Group.

Printed in Scotland for The Stationery Office Limited
J37711, C5, 2/98, CCN 003808